Novena to St. Catherine of Alexandria

Biography, Life, Legacy, Reflections, and 9-Day Powerful Prayers to the Patron Saint of Philosophers, Preachers, Students, Unmarried Girls, & Young Women

FR James Benedict

CONTENTS

A Novena of Strength

A Novena of Strength

St. Catherine of Alexandria, also known as St. Catherine of the Wheel, was a Christian martyr of the early Church. Born in the late 3rd century, her exact birthdate is unclear, but her life and legacy have left an indelible mark on Christian history.

Catherine was born in Alexandria, Egypt, to noble parents. Renowned for her intellect and unwavering Christian faith, she dedicated herself to a life of prayer and study. Legends tell of her debating with pagan scholars and converting many to Christianity through her eloquence and wisdom.

Emperor Maxentius, impressed by her beauty and intellect, sought to marry her. However, Catherine, committed to her vow of virginity and devoted to Christ, refused the emperor's proposal. Angered, Maxentius subjected her to various tortures, including the infamous breaking wheel, but each attempt failed miraculously.

It is said that angels transported Catherine to Mount Sinai during her torture, where she encountered a mystical marriage with Christ. Eventually, she was beheaded around 305 AD for her unyielding faith.

St. Catherine of Alexandria is venerated as one of the Fourteen Holy Helpers and is considered a patron saint of scholars, philosophers, and unmarried women. Her feast day is celebrated on November 25th.

Devotion to St. Catherine has transcended centuries, with numerous churches and monasteries dedicated to her. Artists, inspired by her courage and martyrdom, have depicted her in countless paintings and sculptures.

As we invoke her intercession, let us seek the strength to withstand challenges to our faith and the wisdom to navigate the complexities of life. May St. Catherine's legacy guide us in our pursuit of truth and inspire us to stand firm in our Christian convictions.

St. Catherine of Alexandria, pray for us, that we may emulate your faith, courage, and unwavering commitment to Christ. Amen.

Day One

Novena to St. Catherine of Alexandria

In the name of the Father, and of the Son, and the Holy Spirit.

Amen.

Dear St. Catherine of Alexandria, holy and courageous martyr, we come before you seeking your intercession and guidance. We humbly ask for your powerful intercession to bring our intentions before the throne of God.

St. Catherine, you were known for your unwavering faith, wisdom, and ability to defend the truth fearlessly. Through your prayers and intercession, countless miracles have been attributed to your help. We approach you today with hearts full of trust and hope, seeking your assistance in our time of need.

We ask that you help us grow in faith, deepen our understanding of God's will, and grant us the strength to face any challenges that come our way. We implore you to intercede for us before the Lord, that He may grant our petitions if they align with His divine plan for us.

St. Catherine, we ask for your guidance and protection in all aspects of our lives. Help us to live virtuously, to follow the path of righteousness, and to be a light to others. Inspire us to embrace wisdom and knowledge, just as you did during your earthly life.

We reflect on your virtues and strive to emulate them in our own lives. Help us to cultivate patience, kindness, compassion, and courage. May we learn to stand firm in our beliefs, even when facing adversity.

St. Catherine, we entrust our intentions and desires to your care. Please present them to Jesus, our Lord, and Savior, who is always ready to listen to your pleas on our behalf. We ask that you intercede for (mention your specific intentions here...).

St. Catherine of Alexandria, Pray for us. Amen.

Say 1: Our father…

Say 1: Hail Mary…

Say 1: Glory be…

Day Two

Novena to St. Catherine of Alexandria

In the name of the Father, and of the Son, and the Holy Spirit.

Amen.

Dear St. Catherine of Alexandria, holy and courageous martyr, we come before you seeking your intercession and guidance. We humbly ask for your powerful intercession to bring our intentions before the throne of God.

St. Catherine, you were known for your unwavering faith, wisdom, and ability to

defend the truth fearlessly. Through your prayers and intercession, countless miracles have been attributed to your help. We approach you today with hearts full of trust and hope, seeking your assistance in our time of need.

We ask that you help us grow in faith, deepen our understanding of God's will, and grant us the strength to face any challenges that come our way. We implore you to intercede for us before the Lord, that He may grant our petitions if they align with His divine plan for us.

St. Catherine, we ask for your guidance and protection in all aspects of our lives. Help us to live virtuously, to follow the path of righteousness, and to be a light to others. Inspire us to embrace wisdom and knowledge, just as you did during your earthly life.

We reflect on your virtues and strive to emulate them in our own lives. Help us to cultivate patience, kindness, compassion, and courage. May we learn to stand firm in our beliefs, even when facing adversity.

St. Catherine, we entrust our intentions and desires to your care. Please present them to Jesus, our Lord, and Savior, who is always ready to listen to your pleas on our behalf. We ask that you intercede for (mention your specific intentions here...).

St. Catherine of Alexandria, Pray for us. Amen.

Say 1: Our father...

Say 1: Hail Mary...

Say 1: Glory be...

Day Three

Novena to St. Catherine of Alexandria

In the name of the Father, and of the Son, and the Holy Spirit.

Amen.

Dear St. Catherine of Alexandria, holy and courageous martyr, we come before you seeking your intercession and guidance. We humbly ask for your powerful intercession to bring our intentions before the throne of God.

St. Catherine, you were known for your unwavering faith, wisdom, and ability to

defend the truth fearlessly. Through your prayers and intercession, countless miracles have been attributed to your help. We approach you today with hearts full of trust and hope, seeking your assistance in our time of need.

We ask that you help us grow in faith, deepen our understanding of God's will, and grant us the strength to face any challenges that come our way. We implore you to intercede for us before the Lord, that He may grant our petitions if they align with His divine plan for us.

St. Catherine, we ask for your guidance and protection in all aspects of our lives. Help us to live virtuously, to follow the path of righteousness, and to be a light to others. Inspire us to embrace wisdom and knowledge, just as you did during your earthly life.

We reflect on your virtues and strive to emulate them in our own lives. Help us to cultivate patience, kindness, compassion, and courage. May we learn to stand firm in our beliefs, even when facing adversity.

St. Catherine, we entrust our intentions and desires to your care. Please present them to Jesus, our Lord, and Savior, who is always ready to listen to your pleas on our behalf. We ask that you intercede for (mention your specific intentions here...).

St. Catherine of Alexandria, Pray for us. Amen.

Say 1: Our father...

Say 1: Hail Mary...

Say 1: Glory be...

Day Four

Novena to St. Catherine of Alexandria

In the name of the Father, and of the Son, and the Holy Spirit.

Amen.

Dear St. Catherine of Alexandria, holy and courageous martyr, we come before you seeking your intercession and guidance. We humbly ask for your powerful intercession to bring our intentions before the throne of God.

St. Catherine, you were known for your unwavering faith, wisdom, and ability to

defend the truth fearlessly. Through your prayers and intercession, countless miracles have been attributed to your help. We approach you today with hearts full of trust and hope, seeking your assistance in our time of need.

We ask that you help us grow in faith, deepen our understanding of God's will, and grant us the strength to face any challenges that come our way. We implore you to intercede for us before the Lord, that He may grant our petitions if they align with His divine plan for us.

St. Catherine, we ask for your guidance and protection in all aspects of our lives. Help us to live virtuously, to follow the path of righteousness, and to be a light to others. Inspire us to embrace wisdom and knowledge, just as you did during your earthly life.

We reflect on your virtues and strive to emulate them in our own lives. Help us to cultivate patience, kindness, compassion, and courage. May we learn to stand firm in our beliefs, even when facing adversity.

St. Catherine, we entrust our intentions and desires to your care. Please present them to Jesus, our Lord, and Savior, who is always ready to listen to your pleas on our behalf. We ask that you intercede for (mention your specific intentions here...).

St. Catherine of Alexandria, Pray for us. Amen.

Say 1: Our father...

Say 1: Hail Mary...

Say 1: Glory be...

Day Five

Novena to St. Catherine of Alexandria

In the name of the Father, and of the Son, and the Holy Spirit.

Amen.

Dear St. Catherine of Alexandria, holy and courageous martyr, we come before you seeking your intercession and guidance. We humbly ask for your powerful intercession to bring our intentions before the throne of God.

St. Catherine, you were known for your unwavering faith, wisdom, and ability to

defend the truth fearlessly. Through your prayers and intercession, countless miracles have been attributed to your help. We approach you today with hearts full of trust and hope, seeking your assistance in our time of need.

We ask that you help us grow in faith, deepen our understanding of God's will, and grant us the strength to face any challenges that come our way. We implore you to intercede for us before the Lord, that He may grant our petitions if they align with His divine plan for us.

St. Catherine, we ask for your guidance and protection in all aspects of our lives. Help us to live virtuously, to follow the path of righteousness, and to be a light to others. Inspire us to embrace wisdom and knowledge, just as you did during your earthly life.

We reflect on your virtues and strive to emulate them in our own lives. Help us to cultivate patience, kindness, compassion, and courage. May we learn to stand firm in our beliefs, even when facing adversity.

St. Catherine, we entrust our intentions and desires to your care. Please present them to Jesus, our Lord, and Savior, who is always ready to listen to your pleas on our behalf. We ask that you intercede for (mention your specific intentions here...).

St. Catherine of Alexandria, Pray for us. Amen.

Say 1: Our father...

Say 1: Hail Mary...

Say 1: Glory be...

Day Six
Novena to St. Catherine of Alexandria

In the name of the Father, and of the Son, and the Holy Spirit.

Amen.

Dear St. Catherine of Alexandria, holy and courageous martyr, we come before you seeking your intercession and guidance. We humbly ask for your powerful intercession to bring our intentions before the throne of God.

St. Catherine, you were known for your unwavering faith, wisdom, and ability to

defend the truth fearlessly. Through your prayers and intercession, countless miracles have been attributed to your help. We approach you today with hearts full of trust and hope, seeking your assistance in our time of need.

We ask that you help us grow in faith, deepen our understanding of God's will, and grant us the strength to face any challenges that come our way. We implore you to intercede for us before the Lord, that He may grant our petitions if they align with His divine plan for us.

St. Catherine, we ask for your guidance and protection in all aspects of our lives. Help us to live virtuously, to follow the path of righteousness, and to be a light to others. Inspire us to embrace wisdom and knowledge, just as you did during your earthly life.

We reflect on your virtues and strive to emulate them in our own lives. Help us to cultivate patience, kindness, compassion, and courage. May we learn to stand firm in our beliefs, even when facing adversity.

St. Catherine, we entrust our intentions and desires to your care. Please present them to Jesus, our Lord, and Savior, who is always ready to listen to your pleas on our behalf. We ask that you intercede for (mention your specific intentions here...).

St. Catherine of Alexandria, Pray for us. Amen.

Say 1: Our father...

Say 1: Hail Mary...

Say 1: Glory be...

Day Seven

Novena to St. Catherine of Alexandria

In the name of the Father, and of the Son, and the Holy Spirit.

Amen.

Dear St. Catherine of Alexandria, holy and courageous martyr, we come before you seeking your intercession and guidance. We humbly ask for your powerful intercession to bring our intentions before the throne of God.

St. Catherine, you were known for your unwavering faith, wisdom, and ability to

defend the truth fearlessly. Through your prayers and intercession, countless miracles have been attributed to your help. We approach you today with hearts full of trust and hope, seeking your assistance in our time of need.

We ask that you help us grow in faith, deepen our understanding of God's will, and grant us the strength to face any challenges that come our way. We implore you to intercede for us before the Lord, that He may grant our petitions if they align with His divine plan for us.

St. Catherine, we ask for your guidance and protection in all aspects of our lives. Help us to live virtuously, to follow the path of righteousness, and to be a light to others. Inspire us to embrace wisdom and knowledge, just as you did during your earthly life.

We reflect on your virtues and strive to emulate them in our own lives. Help us to cultivate patience, kindness, compassion, and courage. May we learn to stand firm in our beliefs, even when facing adversity.

St. Catherine, we entrust our intentions and desires to your care. Please present them to Jesus, our Lord, and Savior, who is always ready to listen to your pleas on our behalf. We ask that you intercede for (mention your specific intentions here...).

St. Catherine of Alexandria, Pray for us. Amen.

Say 1: Our father...

Say 1: Hail Mary...

Say 1: Glory be...

Day Eight
Novena to St. Catherine of Alexandria

In the name of the Father, and of the Son, and the Holy Spirit.

Amen.

Dear St. Catherine of Alexandria, holy and courageous martyr, we come before you seeking your intercession and guidance. We humbly ask for your powerful intercession to bring our intentions before the throne of God.

St. Catherine, you were known for your unwavering faith, wisdom, and ability to

defend the truth fearlessly. Through your prayers and intercession, countless miracles have been attributed to your help. We approach you today with hearts full of trust and hope, seeking your assistance in our time of need.

We ask that you help us grow in faith, deepen our understanding of God's will, and grant us the strength to face any challenges that come our way. We implore you to intercede for us before the Lord, that He may grant our petitions if they align with His divine plan for us.

St. Catherine, we ask for your guidance and protection in all aspects of our lives. Help us to live virtuously, to follow the path of righteousness, and to be a light to others. Inspire us to embrace wisdom and knowledge, just as you did during your earthly life.

We reflect on your virtues and strive to emulate them in our own lives. Help us to cultivate patience, kindness, compassion, and courage. May we learn to stand firm in our beliefs, even when facing adversity.

St. Catherine, we entrust our intentions and desires to your care. Please present them to Jesus, our Lord, and Savior, who is always ready to listen to your pleas on our behalf. We ask that you intercede for (mention your specific intentions here...).

St. Catherine of Alexandria, Pray for us. Amen.

Say 1: Our father...

Say 1: Hail Mary...

Say 1: Glory be...

Day Nine

Novena to St. Catherine of Alexandria

In the name of the Father, and of the Son, and the Holy Spirit.

Amen.

Dear St. Catherine of Alexandria, holy and courageous martyr, we come before you seeking your intercession and guidance. We humbly ask for your powerful intercession to bring our intentions before the throne of God.

St. Catherine, you were known for your unwavering faith, wisdom, and ability to

defend the truth fearlessly. Through your prayers and intercession, countless miracles have been attributed to your help. We approach you today with hearts full of trust and hope, seeking your assistance in our time of need.

We ask that you help us grow in faith, deepen our understanding of God's will, and grant us the strength to face any challenges that come our way. We implore you to intercede for us before the Lord, that He may grant our petitions if they align with His divine plan for us.

St. Catherine, we ask for your guidance and protection in all aspects of our lives. Help us to live virtuously, to follow the path of righteousness, and to be a light to others. Inspire us to embrace wisdom and knowledge, just as you did during your earthly life.

We reflect on your virtues and strive to emulate them in our own lives. Help us to cultivate patience, kindness, compassion, and courage. May we learn to stand firm in our beliefs, even when facing adversity.

St. Catherine, we entrust our intentions and desires to your care. Please present them to Jesus, our Lord, and Savior, who is always ready to listen to your pleas on our behalf. We ask that you intercede for (mention your specific intentions here...).

St. Catherine of Alexandria, Pray for us. Amen.

Say 1: Our father...

Say 1: Hail Mary...

Say 1: Glory be...

Made in the USA
Monee, IL
06 December 2024